My Piano Dream

琴夢成真

The Hao Staff (Piano Roll) Sheet Music can help people, especially adults, enjoy playing the piano immediately.

It also serves as a tool to introduce the concept of the Grand Staff to fresh starters.

吉他有六根弦，所以有六綫譜。
鋼琴有黑白鍵，現在也有了郝氏譜！
郝氏黑白鍵譜！
我們都知道熟讀五綫譜需要花很多時間，這令很多人放棄了親自彈奏自己最喜歡的曲子的機會。
郝氏譜清晰顯示每一個音符在鋼琴上的位置，令您可以直接練習彈奏任何曲子，立即實現夢想。

I touched the piano keyboard for the first time about 4 years ago, at age of 40. I tried to learn to read music on the Grand Staff, but found that to be a major block between me and the music I wanted to play. So I intuitively did something for myself – putting music notes on black and white stripes, so that I knew which keys to play – at one glance! Since then I have learned and enjoyed playing a lot of music I like.

Without the "reading problem", playing piano is a lot easier than most people think! So I decided to let others share the wonderful experience, and enjoy the pleasure of playing the piano, much more easily. That's how the Hao Staff company came about. Since our start of business in 2007, many people have benefited from the Hao Staff (Piano Roll) sheet music. I hope it can help you, too.

Jeff   Hong Kong, Feb 2011

Foreword 前言

我四年前（40歲）第一次摸到鋼琴鍵盤。沒有受過系統音樂訓練的我，
發現認讀五線譜的困難成了我學彈鋼琴的主要障礙。我給自己想了個辦法，
把音符放到黑白條橫格上，應該彈哪些鍵就一目了然了。

靠這種方法我彈會了很多我喜歡的曲子。原來彈琴比一般人想像的要
容易得多！於是很自然地決定，要讓大家也能和我一樣，更容易地享受
彈琴的樂趣。這就是郝氏譜公司的來歷。自從2007年開業以來，
"郝氏（黑白鍵）譜"已令很多人受惠！希望它也能幫到你！

郝氏（黑白鍵）譜能幫助大家，尤其是成年人，迅速體驗彈奏鋼琴曲的
樂趣，同時能有效地使人理解五線譜的讀法，為進一步全方位的音樂學習
（包括樂理學習）打下一個好的基礎。

郝佳   2011年2月于香港

Contents 目錄

Hao Staff - a new piano music notation for all

★ grey and white stripes are the black and white keys themselves (extended)
★ wherever the notehead sits, play that key
★ same traditional music notes, fingering, expression, etc.
★ play with right hand for "up stem", and left hand for "down stem" (unless marked otherwise)

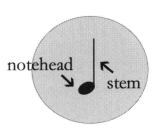

Example - Ode To Joy   (Beethoven)

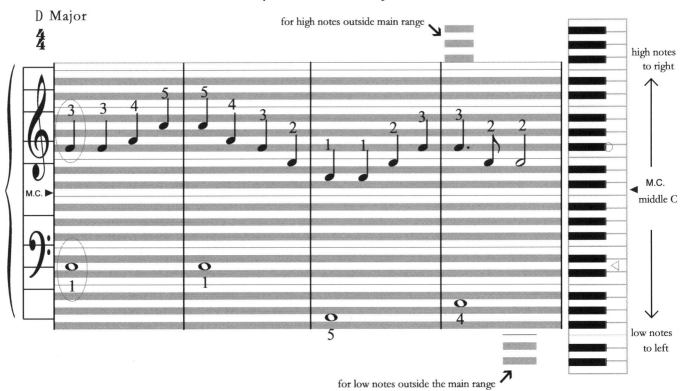

Tips for fast reading :

★ the two blacks (2B) and three blacks (3B) patterns
   repeat themselves
★ find the right keys to play according to where the
   noteheads are in relation to the 2B+3B pattern

Try It Out !

Start playing this song using finger 1
of left hand and 3 of right hand

If next note is "higher", find it to the right
If next note is "lower", find it to the left

Play through note by note a few times
See how fast you improve each time

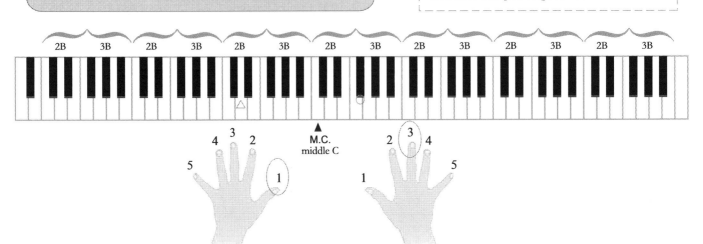

The Hao Staff User Guide

➤ The Hao Staff is a new STAFF ONLY, taking the Grand Staff's place. All the common music notations (e.g. time signatures such as 4/4, music notes of different time values such as semi-breves ○, minims ♩, crotchets ♩, quavers ♪, semi-quavers ♫, etc., ties and dots, rests - 𝄽 𝄾 𝄿 etc., dynamics, and various mood or performance directions, ornaments and embellishments, etc.) are used on the Hao Staff in the same way.

➤ Of course, the most annoying signs - sharp signs (♯), double sharp signs (𝄪), flat signs (♭), double flat signs (𝄫), naturals (♮), and Key signatures (multiples of sharp signs or flat signs) will never appear again.

➤ There is one special "house rule" for notation on the Hao Staff. Unless specifically indicated by "l.h." (Left Hand) or "r.h." (Right Hand) to the contrary, all notes played by the right hand (usually higher notes) will have their stems pointing upward. All notes played by the left hand (usually lower notes) will have their stems pointing downward.

➤ Finger indications are the same as the norm for the Grand Staff sheet music – for both hands, "1" represents the thumb, "2" represents the index finger, "3" represents the middle finger, and so on.

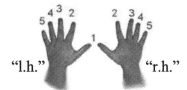

"l.h."　　　"r.h."

➤ Learn to identify keys focusing on "black & white part" of the keyboard. The "black & white part" of the keyboard is identical to the Hao Staff's "gray & white" key stripes. Those who have already learned to play the piano using the Grand Staff tend to form a habit of focusing on the "all white part" of the keyboard. That may give them some problems initially when trying the Hao Staff. Once one realizes this problem, it is not that difficult to make a forced adjustment. And before long, the following image of the keyboard will be engraved in your mind. Matching notes to piano keys becomes automatic.

➤ Following on from the previous point – one should IDENTIFY keys focusing on the "black & white part" of the keyboard. But that does not mean that one only touches (when playing the notes) the narrow parts of the white keys. The best way to play different keys depends on the actual situation. A beginner would, of course, benefit from a tutor's advice in this respect, and acquire the "working rules" in the process.

➤ During the initial stage of using the Hao Staff, one may need to use the Middle C (the C key nearest to the center of the keyboard, which corresponds to the C key stripe in the center of the Hao Staff) as a reference, assisted by the Octave Brackets on the right. This would quickly become unnecessary, as one becomes familiar with the Hao Staff in relation to the keyboard.

➤ If the next note to play is "miles away" in pitch distance, do not try to find it by counting the number of keys from the preceding note. Find it by skipping over "2 blacks", "3 blacks", "2 + 3 blacks" (octave), and so on.

郝氏譜 - 傳承五線譜與音樂傳統的普及型鋼琴譜

★ 灰色和白色的譜條與鍵盤的黑鍵和白鍵一一對應
★ 音符的"符頭"所在的譜條即為應彈奏的黑或白鍵
★ 音符、時值、指法、表情等各種標註均沿用五線譜傳統
★ 音符的"符桿"向上為右手，向下為左手（特殊情況除外：R.H.右手，L.H.左手）

曲譜示例 - 歡樂頌 （貝多芬）

 快速找音訣竅：

★ 灰色譜條及鍵盤的"兩黑"、"三黑"是
　完全重複排列的。

★ 根據符頭與"兩黑"、"三黑"灰色譜條之間的
　位置關係，可快速為音符在鍵盤上定位。

快試彈一下吧

用左手的 1 指 和右手的 3 指開始彈

下一個音更"高"，向右找
下一個音更"低"，向左找

先慢慢一個音一個音地彈幾遍
看看你進步得有多快！

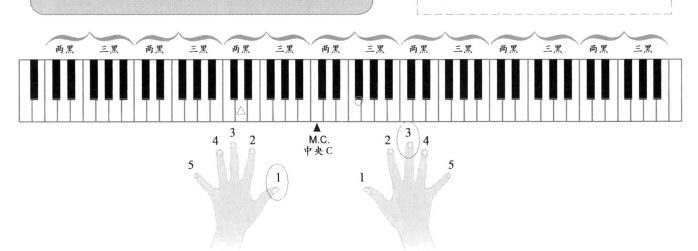

郝氏（黑白鍵）譜使用說明

➢ 郝氏譜是一種新型的"譜"。所有的廣爲採用的音符、標誌等各種符號（如拍號、不同時值的音符，如全音符 o、半音符 ♩、四分音符 ♩、八分音符 ♪、十六分音符 ♪ 等，連接線、符點、休止符，如 - ξ ♪ ♪ 等，強弱符號、感情符號、特殊奏法，等等）的用法都保留它們在五線譜中常規的用法。

➢ 當然，那些最令人頭痛的符號，即升號 (♯)、重升號 (×)、降號 (♭)、重降號 (♭♭)、還原號 (♮)、還有各種調號（由多個升號或降號組成）再也不會出現了。

➢ 另外，郝氏譜也採用了一個特別的規則。除非特別標注了 "L.H.或 l.h."（左手）或 "R.H. 或 r.h."（右手），所有用右手彈奏的音符（通常都是些較高的音）的符幹都向上，所有用左手彈奏的音符（通常都是些較低的音）的符幹都向下。

➢ 指法標記與五線譜一樣，不管是左手還是右手，"1" 代表大拇指；"2" 代表食指；"3" 代表中指；"4" 代表無名指；"5" 代表小拇指。

➢ 在尋找琴鍵時，養成將目光集中在鍵盤的"黑白部分"的習慣。因爲鍵盤的"黑白部分"與郝氏譜的"深灰與白色"的音條"軌道"完全相同。有些習慣用五線譜的人通常喜歡把目光集中在鍵盤的"全白部分"，在剛接觸郝氏譜時可能會因此而不適應。沒關係。一旦意識到這個問題，做一個有意識的調整並不難。不久，以下的鍵盤的圖像就會印在腦子裏。那時，眼看著音符手就會自動找到琴鍵。

➢ 值得一提的是，雖然前邊提到在找琴鍵時要將目光放在鍵盤的"黑白部分"，但這並不是說我們在彈白色的鍵時只去彈它上端夾在黑鍵之間的最窄的那部分。彈琴鍵的哪一部分應看具體的情況而定。初學者應該跟從老師的指導，並逐步找到規律。

➢ 剛接觸郝氏譜時，利用"中央 C"和右邊的"八度括弧"來定位。鋼琴的中央 C 對應的正是郝氏譜的正中的 C 音條。隨著直覺的培養與形成，一般人很快就無需再這樣做。

➢ 如果接下來要彈的音和剛彈的上一個音相差很遠，不要一個鍵一個鍵地去數它們之間的距離。找下一個音的方法是"跳兩黑"、"跳三黑"、或"跳兩加三黑"（八度）等等。

Moonlight Sonata

Piano Sonata No. 14 (Op. 27, No. 2), 1st Movement, in #C Minor

貝多芬 – "月光"奏鳴曲

Beethoven

6 = #C

Moonlight Sonata
Piano Sonata No. 14 (Op. 27, No. 2), 1st Movement, in #C Minor
貝多芬 –"月光"奏鳴曲

una corda

Moonlight Sonata

Piano Sonata No. 14 (Op. 27, No. 2), 1st Movement, in #C Minor

貝多芬 －"月光"奏鳴曲

Moonlight Sonata

Piano Sonata No. 14 (Op. 27, No. 2), 1st Movement, in #C Minor

貝多芬 – "月光"奏鳴曲

Moonlight Sonata
Piano Sonata No. 14 (Op. 27, No. 2), 1st Movement, in #C Minor

貝多芬 – "月光"奏鳴曲

Moonlight Sonata
Piano Sonata No. 14 (Op. 27, No. 2), 1st Movement, in #C Minor
贝多芬 – "月光"奏鸣曲

Moonlight Sonata
Piano Sonata No. 14 (Op. 27, No. 2), 1st Movement, in #C Minor
貝多芬 － "月光"奏鳴曲

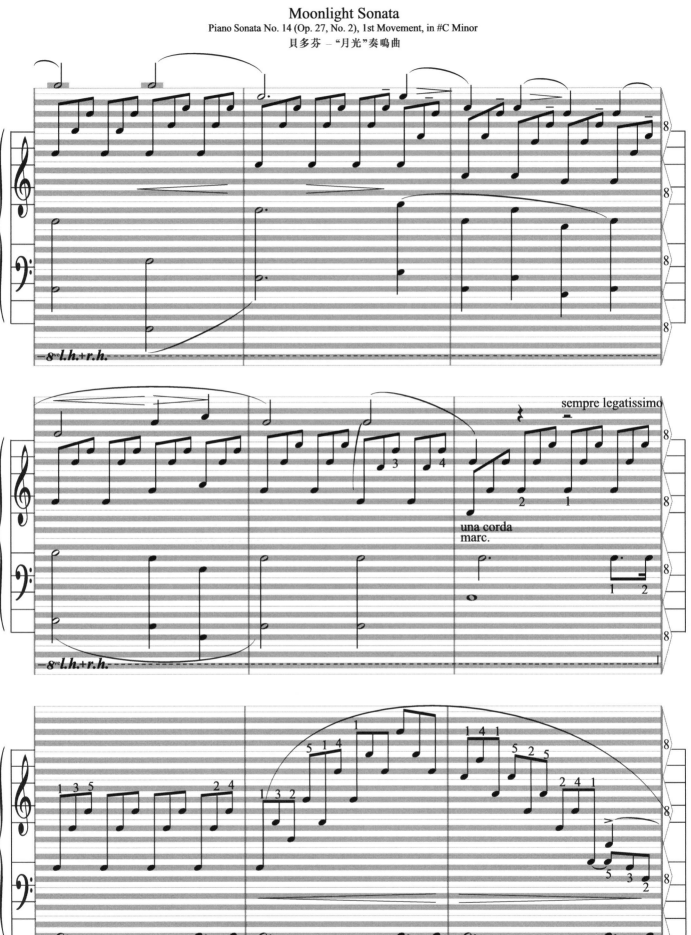

Moonlight Sonata
Piano Sonata No. 14 (Op. 27, No. 2), 1st Movement, in #C Minor
貝多芬 – "月光"奏鳴曲

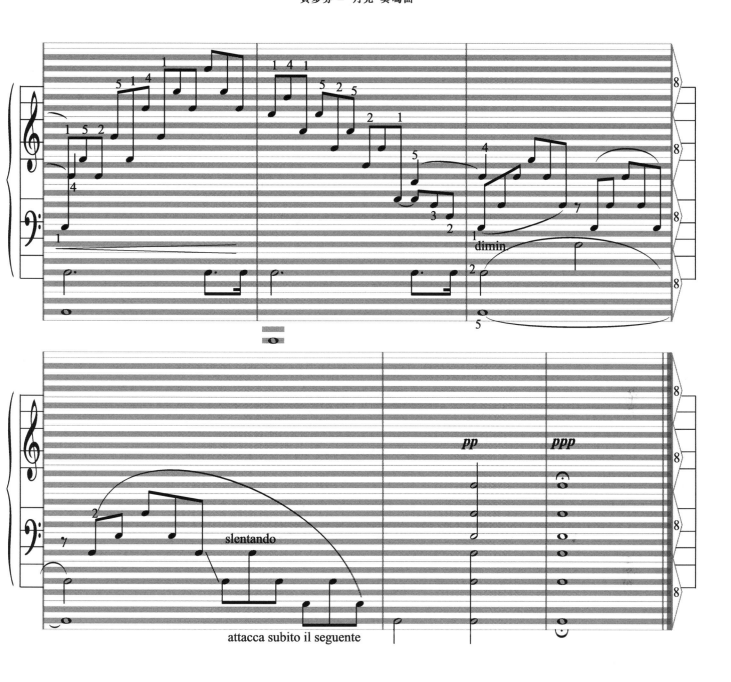

Chopin – Étude Tristesse Op.10 No.3 (Most Loved Part)
Chopin thought this was the most beautiful melody of all he wrote ...
蕭邦 – "離別"練習曲 Op.10 No.3 (最動聽部分)
蕭邦自己認為這是他所作的最為動聽的旋律 …

My Piano Dream **2**
琴 夢 成 真

ISBN 978-988-18935-2-9

Für Elise (Part I)

貝多芬 – 致愛麗絲（最著名部份）

Beethoven

6 = A

Für Elise (Part I)
貝多芬 – 致愛麗絲（最著名部份）

Pachelbel – Canon in D Major
With the repeating chord progression of the left hand, and the progressive buildup of the
right hand, it is a great piece for the beginners to have fun with.

帕赫貝爾 – D大調卡農曲
左手的和弦進行不停地重複，循序漸進，演繹出各種每妙的音階，非常適合初學者。

Hisaishi – Castle In The Sky (Innocent)
This version is made extremely popular on the internet by Paul Li's recording in 2006.
He clarified in his blog that it was arranged by "fxystudio" of http://popiano.org.

久石讓 – 《天空之城》电影插曲 (純真)
這個版本由於李家祥2006年的錄音在互聯網迅速走紅。他在自己的博客澄清，
改編者是 http://popiano.org 的"fxystudio"。

My Piano Dream **3**
琴 夢 成 真

ISBN 978-988-18935-3-6

Chase

Allegro Vivente (♩=80)

1 = C

米亞斯可夫斯基 – 追逐

Miaskovsky

Minuet

莫札特 — 小步舞曲

Mozart

1 = C

Lovely Spring - K596

莫札特 – 渴望春天 K596

Mozart

1 = F

Leicht bewegt (♩.=69)

Lovely Spring - K596

莫札特 – 渴望春天

Mozart – Turkish March (Sonata K.331, 3rd Mov.)
Unmistakably one of Mozart's most famous and popular piano sonatas.

莫札特 – 土耳其進行曲

幾乎可以肯定，你不只一次聽到過這首曲子，這是莫札特最受歡迎的鋼琴奏鳴曲之一。

My Piano Dream 琴夢成真 4

ISBN 978-988-18935-4-3

Melody

舒曼 – 旋律

Robert Schumann

1 = C

Moderato (♩=92)

Melody

舒曼 – 旋律

Study Op.139 No.36

車爾尼 – 練習曲 Op.139 No.36

Czerny

Study Op.139 No.36

車爾尼 – 練習曲

Silent Night

平安夜

Original German lyrics Joseph Mohr
English Translation John F. Young

Original Music Franz Gruber
Arranged for easy piano by Jeff Hao

Silent Night
平安夜

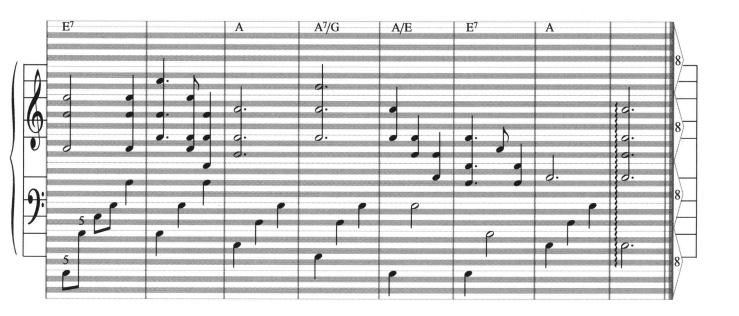

Lyrics

1.

Silent night, holy night
All is calm, all is bright
'Round young virgin, mother and child
Holy infant so tender and mild
Sleep in heavenly peace
Sleep in heavenly peace

2.

Silent night, holy night
Shepherds quake at the sight
Glories stream from heaven a far
Heavenly hosts sing Alleluia
Christ the Savior is born
Christ the Savior is born

3.

Silent night, holy night
Son of God, at the sight
Radiant beams from Thy holy face
With the dawn of redeeming grace
Jesus, Lord, at Thy birth
Jesus, Lord, at Thy birth

German Folk Song

巴赫－德国民歌

J.S.Bach

Note: Use staccato for notes not slurred.

Impromptu on C7 (Ernie Walking Home)

郝佳 – C7上的小即興（恩尼步行回家）

Jeff Hao

1 = C　♩ = 132

Lively

Impromptu on C7 (Ernie Walking Home)

郝佳 – C7上的小即興 (恩尼步行回家)

Impromptu on C7 (Ernie Walking Home)

郝佳 – C7上的小即興（恩尼步行回家）

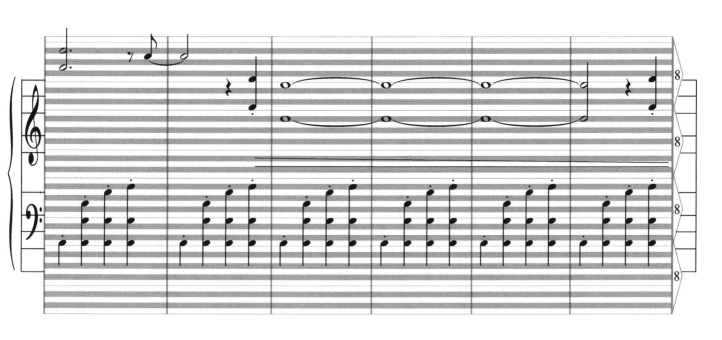

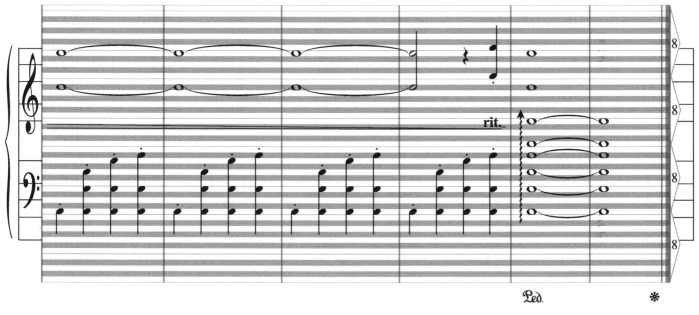

Can Play A Little Bit

羅宇桑 – 會彈一點點

Y.W. Law

1 = C

♩ = 135

Can Play A Little Bit

羅宇榮 – 會彈一點點

Can Play A Little Bit

羅宇桀 – 會彈一點點

Can Play A Little Bit
羅宇桑 – 會彈一點點

For You I Would

王菲 – 我願意

曲：黃國倫
詞：姚謙
改編：Jeff Hao 郝佳

1 = D

♩=80
Quietly

4/4

For You I Would

王菲 — 我願意

For You I Would

王菲 – 我願意

思念是一種很玄的東西，如影， 隨形。無聲又無息，出沒在心底，轉眼，吞沒我在寂默裏。

我無力抗拒，特別是夜裏，喔，想你到無法呼吸。恨不能立即，朝你狂奔去，大聲的告訴你 ...

願意爲你，我願意爲你，我願意爲你，忘記我姓名。就算多一秒，停留在你懷裏，失去世界也不可惜。

我願意爲你，我願意爲你，我願意爲你，被放逐天際。只要你真心，拿愛與我回應，

什麼都願意，什麼都願意，爲你。

Hello, I Love You
(Won't You Tell Me Your Name?)

大門樂隊 The Doors — 喂，我愛你（告訴我你的名字）

Words and Music by
THE DOORS

1 = A

♩=110

Hello, I Love You
(Won't You Tell Me Your Name?)
大門樂隊 The Doors — 喂，我愛你（告訴我你的名字）

Hello, I Love You
(Won't You Tell Me Your Name?)
大門樂隊 The Doors — 喂，我愛你（告訴我你的名字）

Hello, I Love You
(Won't You Tell Me Your Name?)
大門樂隊 The Doors — 喂，我愛你（告訴我你的名字）

Hello, I Love You
(Won't You Tell Me Your Name?)

大門樂隊 The Doors — 喂，我愛你（告訴我你的名字）

Repeat and fade to end

"*Without music life would be a mistake.*" – **Friedrich Nietzsche**

"沒有音樂的生命是一個錯誤。" – 弗里德里希·尼采

Special thanks to Ms. GAN Qi, Ms. Cecilia Li, and Mr. ZHU Tao

Designed by ingDesign Consultants/ www.ingdesign.com.hk

First published and distributed in 2011 by
Hao Staff Music Publishing (Hong Kong) Company Limited
Tel : (852) 6291 0501
Fax: (852) 3011 9931
Email: info@haostaff.com
Website: www.haostaff.com
11/F, AXA Center, 151 Gloucester Road, Wanchai, Hong Kong

特別鳴謝：甘琦女士、李抒青女士、朱濤先生

設計：ingDesign Consultants/ www.ingdesign.com.hk

郝氏譜音樂出版 (香港) 有限公司出版、發行，初版2011
電話：(852) 6291 0501
傳真：(852) 3011 9931
電郵：info@haostaff.com
網站：www.haostaff.com
香港灣仔告士打道151號國衛中心11層

Made in the USA
San Bernardino, CA
20 March 2018